# The Highest Mountains In The World

## Geology for Children
## Children's Earth Sciences Books

**BABY PROFESSOR**

EDUCATION KIDS

Speedy Publishing LLC
40 E. Main St. #1156
Newark, DE 19711
www.speedypublishing.com

In this book, we're going to cover the fourteen highest mountains in the world. So, let's get right to it!

Mount Everest

Would you like to scale the highest mountains in the world? To be a successful mountain climber you'll need to be in excellent physical shape. You'll need to know how to navigate using a map and how to administer first aid to injured team members. In addition to these skills, you'll need to be extremely focused and mentally stable. You'll also need to have a lot of perseverance.

All of the highest mountains in the world are located in Asia and many of them are located in the country of Nepal. Mountains can be measured in several different ways. The mountains in this book are all in the "eight-thousander" club because they are over 8,000 meters high. Let's go on a journey to visit each of these majestic mountains!

Valley of the Ten Peaks, Canadian Rockies

# MOUNT EVEREST
## 29,035 feet

Beautiful Mount Everest is the highest mountain in the world. Rising 8,850 meters, it's part of the Himalayan range and is situated on the border of the Sagarmatha Zone in the country of Nepal and the countries of Tibet and China.

Compared to many of the other mountains in this list, Mount Everest is easier to climb. However, that doesn't mean that it isn't dangerous. Many climbers of both advanced and amateur climbing skill have tackled this immense mountain and many have unfortunately died trying.

Quick changes in the weather and wind, subzero temperatures and the high altitude makes this long mountainous climb very difficult.

Mount Everest

The terrain is simpler than the mountains of K2 or the peak of Nanga Parbat. The first successful climb by Edmund Hillary and Tenzing Norgay took place in 1953. More than 600 mountain climbers have tried to climb Everest and at least 100 have died in the process.

**K2**
**28,250 feet**

The second-highest mountain in the world, K2, also called Mount Godwin-Austen, is situated between China and Pakistan and, like Everest, is also part of the Himalayas.

It's actually a far more dangerous climb than climbing Everest. Out of those who attempt to scale this 8,611-meter peak, 25% never return again and die somewhere on the mountain.

Its mortality rate is the third highest in this top ten list. The Italian expedition of Achille Compagnoni and Lino Lacedelli were the first to reach its treacherous summit in 1954.

# KANGCHENJUNGA
## 28,169 feet

At one time, it was believed to be the mountain that was highest, but at a height of 8,586 meters, Kangchenjunga is the third highest peak in the world.

The unusual name of this mountain translates to "The Five Treasures of the Snow." This mountain is considered holy by believers of the Kirat Mundhum, a religion that combines animism, the worship of ancestors, and Tibetan Buddhism.

It's thought by believers that each peak represents sacred gifts from nature and their holy ancestors, such as sacred books, life-giving grain, the metals, gold and silver, and precious gems.

When the first expedition scaled the mountain in 1955, the British climbers George Band and Joe Brown stopped a few meters away from the summit out of respect for these believers.

This tradition has been honorably kept by most expeditions that have scaled this amazing mountain.

# LHOTSE
## 27,920 feet

The fourth highest
mountain peak on
Earth is Lhotse
and it's attached
to Mount Everest
at the South Col.

The South Col is a very sharp-edged pass between the two mountains and when climbers attempt Everest from the southeast direction, their final camp before the summit is located at South Col. South Col, which never drops below 8,000 meters, is usually swept by very high winds so it doesn't have much accumulation of snow, making it a good site for the night. Lhotse has the steepest mountain face that covers an area of about 2 miles by 1.5 miles.

Many climbers have attempted to scale this steep face. Very few have succeeded to reach the summit from this face and many have died. The summit was first reached by a Swiss team, Ernst Reiss and Fritz Luchsinger in 1956.

**MAKALU**
27,765 feet

The fifth highest mountain peak, Makalu is situated on the border of China and Nepal, about 14 miles directly east of Everest.

With a height of 8,463 meters, this majestic mountain has a peak that stands out due to its shape, which looks like a pyramid with four sides. Another high peak called Kangchungtse, also called Makulu II, is situated northeast of Makulu's main summit.

It's connected to Makalu through Chomo Lonzo, which is a saddle between the two mountains. Makalu was first climbed by J. Franco's French Expedition in 1955.

Cho Oyu

# CHO OYU
## 26,906 feet

Standing at 8,201 meters high, Cho Oyu is considered to be the sixth highest mountain. Mountains that are at least 8,000 meters high, including all the mountains in this book, are called "eight-thousanders." Cho Oyu is known as the easiest of all these "eight-thousanders" to climb.

Like most of the other mountains in this group, it straddles Nepal and the country of Tibet. Its name means "Turquoise Goddess" in the native Tibetan language.

Climbers use Cho Oyu as a warm up for the more challenging climb of Everest. The first expedition to reach the summit in 1954 was from Austria and included Herbert Tichy, Joseph Joechler, and Sherpa Pasang Dawa Lama.

# DHAULAGIRI
## 26,794 feet

At 8,167 meters high, Dhaulagiri, whose name means "White Mountain" is situated due north of central Nepal.

Both the south and west faces of this mountain each rise up 4000 meters from the mountain's base and have very steep drops. The most daring climbers attempt these faces but often fail. Along with another mountain peak in this list, Annapurna, Dhaulagiri makes a spectacular scene. The two mountains are situated face to face with a beautiful valley between them. The first climbers to get to the top of Dhaulagiri were a team representing Switzerland and Austria in 1960.

Dhaulagiri

# MANASLU
## 26,758 feet

The high peak of the Gurkha massif, the name of this mountain translates to "Mountain of the Spirit."

At a height of 8,156 meters, Manaslu is considered to be the eighth highest peak. It is part of the Nepalese Himalayan mountain range and its extended ridges as well as its valley glaciers are accessible from all directions to skilled climbers.

From a distance, its peak rises up dramatically from the surrounding landscape. A Japanese Expedition with climbers named T. Imanishi and Gyalzen Norbu were the first to get there in 1956.

# NANGA PARBAT
## 26,658 feet

The ninth mountain in the list of fourteen, Nanga Parbat towers 8,125 meters high. Although its name means "Naked Mountain" in the Urdu language, it is known by many climbers as Killer Mountain due to the fact that the climb to the summit is so dangerous. The mountain's dramatic summit towers above the surrounding lands in the country of Pakistan. The first successful climber of this summit was Herman Buhl in 1953.

Annapurna

# ANNAPURNA
## 26,545 feet

Annapurna is not just one peak, it's a series of peaks with the highest being Annapurna I. Situated in the central region of Nepal, it rises just over 8,090 meters high. Climbing this mountain is not for the faint of heart. Its peaks are some of the most deadly for climbers. Forty percent of the climbers who try die during their attempts. A French Expedition with climbers Maurice Herzog and Louis Lachenal were the first to reach its summit in 1950.

GASHERBRUM I

26,470 feet

# BROAD PEAK
## 26,400 feet

Gasherbrum I, Broad Peak, and Gasherbrum II are all peaks in a remote group of high peaks called Gasherbrum. They are situated in the Karakoram mountain range and they form a half circle around their own glacier, named South Gasherbrum Glacier.

The shapes of these peaks make them look like pyramids with steep walls and jagged, rugged ridges. Gasherbrum I is also known as Hidden Peak because it is so remote. Three of the peaks in this compact range of mountains are over 8,000 meters high. Gasherbrum I is at number 11 of our list of 14 in height, Broad Peak is at number 12 and Gasherbrum II is at number 13. The first to reach this group's summit was Clinch's American Expedition with climbers Pete Schoening and Andy Kauffman in 1958.

Broad Peak

# SHISHA PANGMA
## 26,289 feet

The lowest mountain in the "eight thousander club" Shisha Pangma is still a massive mountain. It has a steep, rugged face. The highest peak of the range of mountains called Langtang Himal and it towers over its companion peaks. It was the last of the mountains in this group to be climbed. It is located on the Tibetan side of the border of Kathmandu, which is the capital city of Nepal. The summit was reached in 1964 by Hsu Ching and his ten-man Chinese Expedition team.

Buck Mountain

Awesome! Now you know a lot about the highest mountains in the world. You can find more Earth Science and Geology Books from Baby Professor by searching the website of your favorite book retailer.

Made in the USA
Monee, IL
16 April 2020